ANIMALS IN THEIR WORLD

A SHIVER OF SHARKS
AND OTHER OCEAN ANIMAL GROUPS

Tracy Nelson Maurer

TABLE OF CONTENTS

- Animal Groups 3
- Glossary 22
- Index 23

A Crabtree Seedlings Book

ANIMAL GROUPS

Many words for groups of animals , such as pride of lions, came from kings and queens hundreds of years ago. They made up fun and fancy ways of speaking to separate themselves from common folks.

Carl Linnaeus
1707 – 1778

Carl Linnaeus developed a system for naming and grouping living things in the 1730s. Scientists still use his ideas today.

Carl Linnaeus grouped living things into two kingdoms: plants and animals. Today, scientists group living things into five kingdoms: animals, plants, **fungi**, protists (very simple **organisms**), and **bacteria**.

Sometimes we give animal groups names that are not scientific.

A **smack** of jellyfish bumps into its food.

A jellyfish has no brain, heart, bones, or eyes.

A **run** of salmon swims upstream to **spawn**.

A **pod** of dolphins plays in the waves.

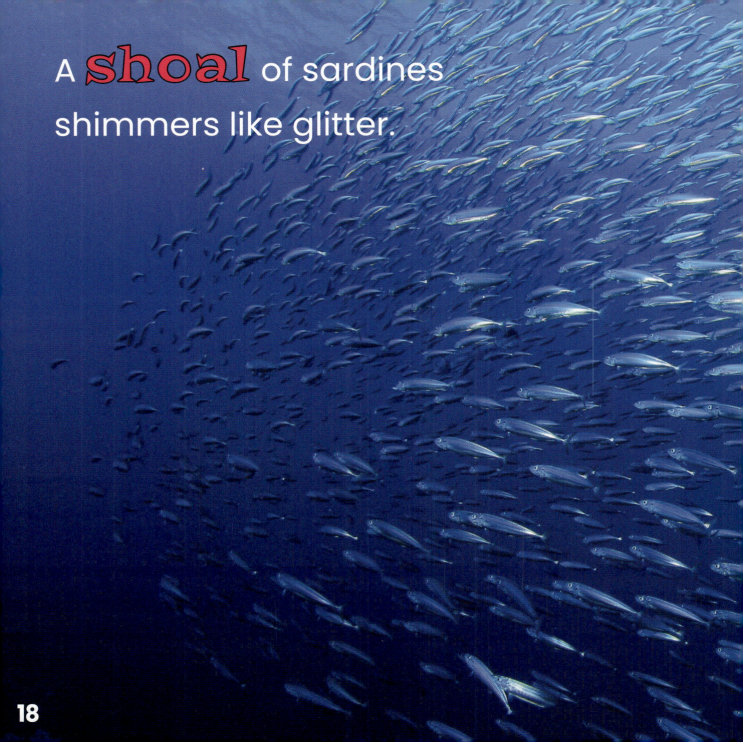

A **shoal** of sardines shimmers like glitter.

Glossary

bacteria (bac-TIHR-ee-uh): Bacteria are microscopic organisms. Some are useful. Others can make you sick.

echolocation (EK-oh-loh-KAY-shun): Echolocation is sending sound waves and using their echoes to figure out where things are.

fungi (FUHNG-gye): Fungi are a group of organisms that include mushrooms and toadstools.

organisms (OR-guh-niz-uhmz): Organisms are anything that is living.

spawn (SPAWN): To spawn is to release a large number of eggs. Fish, frogs, and toads spawn.

species (SPEE-sheez): A species is one certain kind of animal within a group. A sockeye is a species within the salmon group.

Index

dolphins 16
echolocation 16
jellyfish 10
kingdoms 5
Linnaeus, Carl 4, 5
prey 6

salmon 12, 13
sharks 6
species 8
squid 8
stingrays 14

Help keep oceans clean and safe for sharks and other ocean animal groups.

23

School-to-Home Support for Caregivers and Teachers

This book helps children grow by letting them practice reading. Here are a few guiding questions to help the reader build his or her comprehension skills. Possible answers appear here in red.

Before Reading

- **What do I think this book is about?** I think this book is about sharks. I think this book is about sharks all over the world.

- **What do I want to learn about this topic?** I want to learn more about the eating habits of sharks. I want to learn how many teeth sharks have.

During Reading

- **I wonder why...** I wonder why animal groups have strange names. I wonder why a group of sharks is called a shiver.

- **What have I learned so far?** I have learned that many of the words we use to describe animal groups came from kings and queens. I have learned that in the 1730s Carl Linnaeus developed a system for naming and grouping living things.

After Reading

- **What details did I learn about this topic?** I have learned that Sockeye salmon are blue in saltwater and red in freshwater. I have learned that oysters help clean water and protect the coast from storm damage.

- **Read the book again and look for the glossary words.** I see the word *fungi* on page 5, and the word *spawn* on page 12. The other glossary words are found on page 22.

Library and Archives Canada Cataloguing in Publication

Available at the Library and Archives Canada

Library of Congress Cataloging-in-Publication Data

Available at the Library of Congress

Crabtree Publishing Company

www.crabtreebooks.com   1–800–387–7650

Print book version produced jointly with Blue Door Education in 2023

Written by: Tracy Nelson Maurer

Print coordinator: Katherine Berti

Printed in the U.S.A./072022/CG20220201

Content produced and published by Blue Door Education, Melbourne Beach FL USA. This title Copyright Blue Door Education. All rights reserved. No part of this book may be reproduced or utilized in any form or by any means, electronic or mechanical including photocopying, recording, or by any information storage and retrieval system without permission in writing from the publisher.

Photo Credits:

Cover and pages 6-7 © sirtravelalot, page 5 © Boris Mrdja ; girl page 6 © Patrick Foto; pages 8-9 © Kristina Vackova, page 9 boy and page 11 girl ©Rawpixel.com; cover and pages 10-11 © Sophon K; pages 12-13 © Feng Yu; cover and pages 14-15 © Amanda Nicholls; page 16-17 © By Chase Dekker ; page 18-19 © Rich Carey; page 22 bacteria © OlgaReukova, fungi © bob.leccinum.Robert Kozak, page 23 organisms © udaix, spawn © thanaphon Saduakki; page 23 ©2018 Rich Carey; All images from Shutterstock.com except pages 20-21 PamSchodt / istockphoto.com

Published in the United States
Crabtree Publishing
347 Fifth Ave.
Suite 1402-145
New York, NY 10016

Published in Canada
Crabtree Publishing
616 Welland Ave.
St. Catharines, Ontario
L2M 5V6